Table of Contents

Introduction

The introduction of low-fat, high-complex carbohydrate diets far the prevention and treatment of obesity was based on the causal link established between dietary fat and body fatness. Observational and mechanistic studies show that because fat possesses a lower satiating power than carbohydrate and protein, a diet rich in fat can increase energy intake. The propensity to gain weight is enhanced in susceptible persons, particularly sedentary people who have a genetic predisposition to obesity.Low-fat diets cause weight loss proportional to pretreatment body weight in a dose dependent manner; that is, weight loss is correlated positively to the reduction in dietary fat content. A reduction of 10% fat energy produces an average 5-kg weight loss in obese persons. As with traditional caloric counting diets, obese persons lose weight only if they adhere to the prescribed low-fat diet. Failure to achieve a weight loss and to maintain it may be attributed in part to lack of adherence to the diet. After a major weight loss, an ad libitum low-fat diet program appears to be superior to caloric counting in maintaining the weight loss 2 years later. Replacing some fat with protein instead of carbohydrate may increase the weight loss further. Moreover, fat substitutes may make it easier to prevent and treat obesity by making the diet palatable. More randomized, controlled, long-term dietary intervention studies are warranted to identify the optimal diet composition for the treatment of obesity.

low-fat diet

A low-fat diet is an eating plan that is low in total fat, unhealthy fat, and cholesterol. You may need to follow a low-fat diet if you have trouble digesting or absorbing fat. You may also need to follow this diet if you have high cholesterol. You can also lower your cholesterol by increasing the amount of fiber in your diet. Soluble fiber is a type of fiber that helps to decrease cholesterol levels.

What do I need to know about the different types of fat in food?

Limit unhealthy fats. A diet that is high in cholesterol, saturated fat, and trans fat may cause unhealthy cholesterol levels. Unhealthy cholesterol levels increase your risk of heart disease.

Cholesterol: Limit intake of cholesterol to less than 200 mg per day. Cholesterol is found in meat, eggs, and dairy.

Saturated fat: Limit saturated fat to less than 7% of your total daily calories. Ask your dietitian how many calories you need each day. Saturated fat is found in butter, cheese, ice cream, whole milk, and palm oil. Saturated fat is also found in meat, such as beef, pork, chicken skin, and processed meats. Processed meats include sausage, hot dogs, and bologna.

Trans fat: Avoid trans fat as much as possible. Trans fat is used in fried and baked foods. Foods that say trans fat free on the label may still have up to 0.5 grams of trans fat per serving.

Include healthy fats. Replace foods that are high in saturated and trans fat with foods high in healthy fats. This may help to decrease high cholesterol levels.

Monounsaturated fats: These are found in avocados, nuts, and vegetable oils, such as olive, canola, and sunflower oil.

Polyunsaturated fats: These can be found in vegetable oils, such as soybean or corn oil. Omega-3 fats can help to decrease the risk of heart disease. Omega-3 fats are found in fish, such as salmon, herring, trout, and tuna. Omega-3 fats can also be found in plant foods, such as walnuts, flaxseed, soybeans, and canola oil.

What foods should I limit or avoid?

Grains:

Snacks that are made with partially hydrogenated oils, such as chips, regular crackers, and butter-flavored popcorn

High-fat baked goods, such as biscuits, croissants, doughnuts, pies, cookies, and pastries

Dairy:

Whole milk, 2% milk, and yogurt and ice cream made with whole milk

Half and half creamer, heavy cream, and whipping cream

Cheese, cream cheese, and sour cream

Meats and proteins:

High-fat cuts of meat (T-bone steak, regular hamburger, and ribs)

Fried meat, poultry (turkey and chicken), and fish

Poultry (chicken and turkey) with skin

Cold cuts (salami or bologna), hot dogs, bacon, and sausage

Whole eggs and egg yolks

Vegetables and fruits with added fat:

Fried vegetables or vegetables in butter or high-fat sau

as cream or cheese sauces

Fried fruit or fruit served with butter or cream

Fats:

Butter, stick margarine, and shortening

Coconut, palm oil, and palm kernel oil

What foods should I include?

Grains:

Whole-grain breads, cereals, pasta, and brown rice

Low-fat crackers and pretzels

Vegetables and fruits:

Fresh, frozen, or canned vegetables (no salt or low-sodium

Fresh, frozen, dried, or canned fruit (canned in light syi

fruit juice)

Avocado

Low-fat dairy products:

Nonfat (skim) or 1% milk

Nonfat or low-fat cheese, yogurt, and cottage cheese

Meats and proteins:

Chicken or turkey with no skin

Baked or broiled fish

Lean beef and pork (loin, round, extra lean hamburger)

Beans and peas, unsalted nuts, soy products

Egg whites and substitutes

Seeds and nuts

Fats:

Unsaturated oil, such as canola, olive, peanut, soybean, or sunflower oil

Soft or liquid margarine and vegetable oil spread

Low-fat salad dressing

What are some other ways I can decrease fat?

Read food labels before you buy foods. Choose foods that have less than 30% of calories from fat. Choose low-fat or fat-free dairy products. Remember that fat free does not mean calorie free. These foods still contain calories, and too many calories can lead to weight gain.

Trim fat from meat and avoid fried food.Trim all visible fat from meat before you cook it. Remove the skin from poultry. Do not fry meat, fish, or poultry.Bake, roast, boil, or broil these foods instead. Avoid fried foods. Eat a baked potato instead of French fries.Steam vegetables instead of sautéing them in butter.

Add less fat to foods. Use imitation bacon bits on salads and baked potatoes instead of regular bacon bits. Use fat-free or low-fat salad dressings instead of regular dressings. Use low-fat or nonfat butter-flavored topping instead of regular butter or margarine on popcorn and other foods.

How can I decrease fat in recipes?

Replace high-fat ingredients with low-fat or nonfat ones. This may cause baked goods to be drier than usual. You may need to use nonfat cooking spray on pans to prevent food from sticking.

You also may need to change the amount of other ingredients, such as water, in the recipe. Try the following:

- Use low-fat or light margarine instead of regular margarine or shortening.
- Use lean ground turkey breast or chicken, or lean ground beef (less than 5% fat) instead of hamburger.
- Add 1 teaspoon of canola oil to 8 ounces of skim milk instead of using cream or half and half.
- Use grated zucchini, carrots, or apples in breads instead of coconut.
- Use blenderized, low-fat cottage cheese, plain tofu, or low-fat ricotta cheese instead of cream cheese.
- Use 1 egg white and 1 teaspoon of canola oil, or use ¼ cup (2 ounces) of fat-free egg substitute instead of a whole egg.
- Replace half of the oil that is called for in a recipe with applesauce when you bake. Use 3 tablespoons of cocoa powder and 1 tablespoon of canola oil instead of a square of baking chocolate.

How can I increase fiber?

Eat enough high-fiber foods to get 20 to 30 grams of fiber every day. Slowly increase your fiber intake to avoid stomach cramps, gas, and other problems.

Eat 3 ounces of whole-grain foods each day. An ounce is about 1 slice of bread. Eat whole-grain breads, such as whole-wheat bread. Whole wheat, whole-wheat flour, or other whole grains should be listed as the first ingredient on the food label. Replace white flour with whole-grain flour or use half of each in recipes. Whole-grain flour is heavier than white flour, so you may have to add more yeast or baking powder.

Eat a high-fiber cereal for breakfast. Oatmeal is a good source of soluble fiber. Look for cereals that have bran or fiber in the name. Choose whole-grain products, such as brown rice, barley, and whole-wheat pasta.

Eat more beans, peas, and lentils. For example, add beans to soups or salads. Eat at least 5 cups of fruits and vegetables each day. Eat fruits and vegetables with the peel because the peel is high in fiber.

Should I Follow a Fat-Restricted Diet?

This diet may be prescribed for certain conditions that make it difficult for the body to digest fat, such as chronic pancreatitis, gallbladder disease or removal, or gastroparesis.

Fat takes more time to digest, so it can sit in the stomach and cause symptoms like cramping, bloating, nausea, and diarrhea [in these populations]. Restricting fat, therefore, makes the digestive process more comfortable.

This type of diet may also be recommended following surgeries involving the lymphatic system. The goal in restricting fat is to prevent what's called a chyle leak. Chyle is a milky looking fluid that contains lymphatic fluid and fat and is produced in the small intestine during digestion according to UWHealth. It's carried in the lymphatic system, and restricting fat post-surgery helps your body produce less chyle, decreasing the risk of a leak and improving the likelihood of healing.

Another reason you may be on a fat-restricted diet is if you have heart disease, high cholesterol, or high triglycerides (fats in the blood); less commonly these days, it may also be recommended to prevent weight gain for some people.

Fat-restricted diet basics

Usually, a fat-restricted diet limits fat intake to less than 50 grams (g) per day. Fat contains nine calories per gram. So, if you need a total of 2,000 calories per day, this means that only about 22 percent of those calories can be from fat. The rest should be from carbohydrate or protein.That said, the specific number recommended for you will largely depend on your size and calorie needs, says Lynett. The reason you're following this type of diet may also play a role.

The difference between a low-fat and a fat-restricted diet

Fat-restricted" and "low-fat" are different terms for the same thing and are often used interchangeably, even in medical settings, low-fat diets are proposed as a type of weight loss diet, while fat-restriction is used as a diet to control symptoms of a medical condition.

Eating guide for a fat-restricted diet

Below you'll find some general direction for the foods you'll focus on if you're following a fat-restricted diet.

Limit Fat Consumption

This means limiting your intake of saturated and trans fats, which are found in animal sources like meat and dairy, says Lynett, and in processed foods like cake, cookies, and potato chips. And you'll avoid adding fats such as butter or margarine to your foods.

Be Strategic if You Eat Meat

Choose leaner sources of protein, like skinless chicken, turkey breast, or pork loin, recommends Gradney. Legumes like beans, lentils, and dried peas are great vegetarian sources of protein, and they also contain heart-healthy fiber.

Focus on Healthy Fats

Whenever possible, opt for sources of polyunsaturated and monounsaturated fats, like olive oil or avocado (though still in limited amounts). These help lower both inflammation and cholesterol.

Consider Restricting Your Nut Intake

If you are on a fat-restricted diet for a digestive condition, you will want to limit nut and nut butter to 1 ounce per day (or the equivalent of 1 tablespoon for nut butters). Nuts are really easy to overeat, so it's important to watch your portions. If you choose to eat nut butter, limit your consumption of other fats to keep your total intake down.

Fuel Up With Plants

Increase your intake of vegetables, fruits, and whole grains, which are foods that are naturally lower in fat.

Minimize Consumption of Packaged Food

Though this tactic is not specific to a fat-restricted diet, you're best off avoiding refined foods or those high in simple sugars, like white bread, snack foods, and crackers. Even if they are labeled low-fat, these foods are converted into sugar in your body. These will increase your triglyceride levels. While you may not be directly ingesting fat, these foods will contribute to elevating the [unhealthy] fats in your blood.

Suggestions on eating a fat-restricted diet

Read Food Labels Carefully

Lynett recommends looking for the following key phrases on food labels when grocery shopping: low-fat, nonfat, and fat-free. Foods that use nonfat/fat-free or similar labels are required to contain less than 0.5 g of fat per labeled serving, per the U.S. Food and Drug Administration (FDA). (5) Those that are low-fat have 3 g or less of fat. Reduced fat, however, doesn't guarantee something is low in fat or is appropriate for your diet; these foods simply must have 25 percent less fat than their original version.

Don't Eat Too Much Fat at Once

Spread your fat intake throughout the day, advises Lynett. "Saving up" fat for one meal can lead to uncomfortable gastrointestinal symptoms, the exact thing you may be looking to prevent with this diet.

Avoid Fried and Sautéed Foods

Use low-fat cooking methods, such as baking, roasting, broiling, poaching, grilling, boiling, or steaming.

Select Lean Cuts of Meat

Loin and round are examples. "If you can see fat around the meat or marbling, that's a cut you probably shouldn't be eating.

Ask Your Doctor About MCT Oil

For some patients, Lynett might recommend using MCT oil, which stands for medium-chain triglycerides. This type of fat easily absorbs into your bloodstream through your stomach, which means it doesn't require pancreatic enzymes to break it down, she explains. Therefore, it can be a useful addition to your diet if you have a GI condition, as well as if you're trying to gain weight. A paper in Practical Gastroenterology published in February 2017 suggests guidelines for using MCT oil: Avoid consuming more than 4 to 7 tablespoons daily, divide the dose evenly between meals, and mix it into foods and beverages for palatability and to make it easier to take.

Also, Ask About Prescription Pancreatic Enzymes

If you have a pancreatic condition, you may need to take additional prescription pancreatic enzymes, says Lynett. Ask your physician if these are recommended for you.

Be Mindful of Potential Nutrient Deficiencies

A long-term fat-restricted diet can lead to nutrient deficiencies, especially when it comes to the fat-soluble vitamins A, E, D, and K. She recommends patients undergo bloodwork to check on nutrient levels once per year. You may also be advised to take a fast-dissolving or chewable multivitamin, which tends to be better absorbed by those with digestive disease.

Remember Your 'Why'

Keep in mind the reason you're doing a fat-restricted diet in the first place, because this, like all diet changes, can be tough to stick with. For instance, if you're on it for gallbladder disease, you have to keep in mind that deviations from the diet say, eating a special high-fat meal for a holiday may leave you in physical pain.

Take Control of Your Food

Some patients feel stuck when they go out to eat because they have no idea what they can order. Ask how things are prepared and then request accommodations, for example: Please don't butter the bun on my sandwich.

Recipes

Thai red duck with sticky pineapple rice

Ingredients

2 duck breasts, skin removed and discarded

1 tbsp Thai red curry paste

zest and juice 1 lime, plus extra wedges to serve

140g jasmine rice

125ml light coconut milk, from a can

140g frozen peas

50g beansprouts

½ red onion, diced

100g fresh pineapple, cubed

1 red chilli, deseeded and finely chopped

¼ small pack coriander, stalks finely chopped, leaves roughly chopped

Method

Sit a duck breast between 2 sheets of cling film on a chopping board. Use a rolling pin to bash the duck until it is 0.5cm thick. Repeat with the other breast, then put them both in a dish. Mix the curry paste with the lime zest and juice, and rub all over the duck. Leave to marinate at room temperature for 20 mins.

Meanwhile, tip the rice into a small saucepan with some salt. Pour over the coconut milk with 150ml water. Bring to a simmer, then cover the pan, turn the heat down low and cook for 5 more mins. Stir in the peas, then cover, turn the heat off and leave for another 10 mins. Check the rice - all the liquid should be absorbed and the rice cooked through. Boil the kettle, put the beansprouts and red onion in a colander and pour over a kettleful of boiling water. Stir the beansprouts and onion into the rice with the pineapple, chilli and coriander stalks, and some more salt if it needs it, and put the lid back on to keep warm.

Heat a griddle pan and cook the duck for 1-2 mins each side or until cooked to your liking. Slice the duck, stir most of the coriander leaves through the rice with a fork to fluff up, and serve alongside the duck, scattered with the remaining coriander.

Piri-piri prawn wrap

Ingredients

150ml pot soured cream

juice 1 lemon

small pack mint, finely chopped

300g peeled raw king prawns

4 tsp vegetable oil

3 large garlic cloves, crushed

1 bird's-eye chilli, finely chopped (deseeded if you don't like it too hot)

1 tsp paprika

4 large flatbreads

3 red peppers, deseeded and thinly sliced

3 Little Gem lettuces, shredded

Method

Heat oven to 160C/140C fan/gas 3. Mix the soured cream with 1 tbsp lemon juice, the mint and seasoning, cover and put in the fridge. Toss the prawns in 2 tsp oil, 1 tbsp lemon juice, the garlic, chilli, paprika and seasoning. Cover and put to one side. Wrap the breads in foil and put in the oven to warm.

Heat a griddle pan on a medium- high heat. Toss the peppers in the remaining 2 tsp oil, season and cook on the griddle for 5-10 mins until charred and softened (you may need to do this in two batches). Transfer the peppers to an ovenproof dish, cover with foil and put in the oven to keep warm. Add the prawns to the griddle pan and cook for 2-3 mins each side until pink, cooked through and lightly charred. Serve with the warm wraps, lettuce, peppers and soured cream.

Prawn, fennel & rocket risotto

Ingredients

1.2l vegetable stock

1 tbsp olive oil

1 onion, finely chopped

1 large garlic clove, finely chopped

1 small fennel bulb, cored and finely chopped

300g risotto rice

300g peeled raw king prawns

1 lemon, ½ zested and 1 tbsp juice

70g bag rocket

Method

Put the stock in a large saucepan, bring to the boil, then lower to a simmer. Meanwhile, heat the oil in a large saucepan. Add the onion, garlic and fennel, and cook on a low heat for 10 mins until the vegetables have softened but not coloured. Add the rice and stir for 2 mins until the grains are hot and making crackling sounds. Increase the heat to medium and start adding the stock, a ladleful at a time, stirring constantly and making sure the stock has absorbed into the rice before adding the next ladleful.

When the rice is almost cooked, add the prawns, lemon zest and some seasoning. Continue adding stock and cooking for another 3-4 mins until the prawns are pink and the rice is cooked. Remove from the heat and stir through the rocket and lemon juice. Check the seasoning, leave the risotto to sit in the pan for 2 mins, then serve.

Oven-baked fish & chips

Ingredients

800g/ 1lb 12 oz floury potato, scrubbed and cut into chips

2 tbsp olive oil

50g fresh breadcrumb

zest 1 lemon

2 tbsp chopped flat-leaf parsley

4 x 140g/5oz thick sustainable white fish fillets

200g/ 7oz cherry tomato

Method

Heat oven to 220C/200C fan/gas 7. Pat chips dry on kitchen paper, then lay in a single layer on a large baking tray. Drizzle with half the olive oil and season with salt. Cook for 40 mins, turning after 20 mins, so they cook evenly.

Mix the breadcrumbs with the lemon zest and parsley, then season well.Top the cod evenly with the breadcrumb mixture, then drizzle .0with the remaining oil. Put in a roasting tin with the cherry tomatoes, then bake in the oven for the final 10 mins of the chips' cooking time.

Chicken, edamame & ginger pilaf

Ingredients

2 tbsp vegetable oil

1 onion, thinly sliced

thumb-sized piece ginger, grated

1 red chilli, deseeded and finely sliced

3 skinless chicken breasts, cut into bite-sized pieces

250g basmati rice

600ml vegetable stock

100g frozen edamame / soya beans

coriander leaves and fat-free Greek yoghurt (optional), to serve

Method

Heat the oil in a medium saucepan, then add the onion, ginger and chilli, along with some seasoning. Cook for 5 mins, then add the chicken and rice. Cook for 2 mins more, then add the stock and bring to the boil. Turn the heat to low, cover and cook for 8-10 mins until the rice is just cooked. During the final 3 mins of cooking, add the edamame beans. Sprinkle some coriander leaves on top and serve with a dollop of Greek yogurt, if you like.

Spiced turkey with bulgur & pomegranate salad

Ingredients

2 tbsp each chopped dill, parsley and mint

zest and juice 1 lemon

1 tbsp harissa paste

500g/1lb 2oz turkey

breast fillets

2 tbsp white wine or water

250g pack bulgur wheat or a mix- we used quinoa and bulgur mix

2 tomatoes, chopped

½ cucumber, diced

100g pack pomegranate

seeds

Method

Heat oven to 200C/180C fan/gas 6. Mix together half the herbs, half the lemon zest and juice, and all the harissa with some seasoning. Rub the turkey in the marinade and leave for 5 mins (or up to 24 hrs in the fridge).

Lay out a large sheet of foil. Put the turkey and marinade, and wine or water, on top, then cover with another layer of foil, fold and crimp the edges to seal. Transfer the parcel to a tray, then bake for 30 mins until cooked through.

Meanwhile, make the salad. Cook the bulgur following pack instructions. Drain, then mix with the remaining herbs, lemon zest and juice, plus the tomatoes, cucumber and pomegranate seeds. Slice the turkey and serve on top of the salad with the foil parcel juices poured on top.

Chilli pepper pumpkin with Asian veg

Ingredients

1 small pumpkin

or ½ butternut squash, cut into chunks (seeds removed), no need to peel

2 tsp sunflower or vegetable oil

1 tsp each mild chilli powder and five spice powder

175g thin-stemmed broccoli

175g bok choi, quartered

2 tbsp low-sodium soy sauce

2 tbsp rice wine vinegar

1 tbsp honey

1 lime, ½ juice, ½ cut into wedges

few coriander leaves

Method

Heat oven to 220C/200C fan/gas 7. Toss the pumpkin in the oil, then sprinkle on the chilli powder, five-spice, 1 tsp black pepper and a pinch of salt, and mix well. Tip into a roasting tray in a single layer and cook for 25-30 mins until tender and starting to caramelise around the edges.

About 5 mins before the pumpkin is cooked, heat a wok or large frying pan and add the broccoli plus 1-2 tbsp water. Cook for 2-3 mins, then add the bok choi, soy, vinegar and honey, and cook for a further 2-3 mins until the veg is tender. Add the lime juice, then divide between 2 plates with the pumpkin, coriander leaves and lime wedges.

Summer pea pasta

Ingredients

3 tbsp olive oil

3 fat garlic cloves, finely chopped

1 red chilli, deseeded and finely chopped

zest 2 lemons

400g pasta

200g fresh or frozen peas

20g pack basil

Method

Heat 1 tbsp oil in a frying pan and cook the garlic and chilli for a couple of mins until very lightly golden. Stir in the zest.

Cook the pasta, adding the peas for the final 2 mins. Drain, then tip everything back into the saucepan. Tip in the garlic, chilli and lemon, scraping in any bits stuck to the pan. Tear in the basil, season and add the remaining olive oil. Stir well.

Miso steak

Ingredients

2 tbsp brown miso paste

1 tbsp dry sherry or sake

1 tbsp caster sugar

2 crushed garlic cloves

300g/11oz lean steak

baby spinach, sliced cucumber, celery, radish and toasted sesame seeds, to serve

Method

Tip the miso paste, Sherry or sake, sugar and garlic into a sealable food bag. Season with a generous grinding of black pepper, then squash it all together until completely mixed. Add the steak, gently massage the marinade into the steak until completely coated, then seal the bag. Pop the bag into the fridge and leave for at least 1 hr, but up to 2 days is fine.

To cook, heat a heavy-based frying pan, griddle pan or barbecue until very hot. Wipe the excess marinade off the steak, then sear for 3 mins on each side for medium-rare or a few mins longer if you prefer the meat more cooked. Set aside for 1 min to rest. Carve the beef into thick slices and serve with a crunchy salad made with the spinach, cucumber, celery, radish and sesame seeds.

Low-fat roasties

Ingredients

800g roasting potatoes, quartered

1 garlic clove, sliced

200ml vegetable stock (from a cube is fine)

2 tbsp olive oil

Method

Heat oven to 200C/fan 180C/gas 6. Put the potatoes and garlic in a roasting tin. Pour over the stock, then brush the tops of the potatoes with half the olive oil. Season, then cook for 50 mins. Brush with the remaining oil and cook 10-15 mins more until the stock is absorbed and the potatoes have browned and cooked through.

Creamy linguine with ham, lemon & basil

Ingredients

400g linguine or spaghetti

90g pack prosciutto

1 tbsp olive oil

juice 1 lemon

2 egg yolks

3 tbsp crème fraîche

large handful basil leaves

large handful grated parmesan, plus extra to serve, if you like

Method

Cook the linguine. Meanwhile, tear the ham into small pieces and fry in the olive oil until golden and crisp.

Drain the pasta, reserving a little of the cooking water, then return to the pan. Tip in the cooked ham. Mix together the lemon juice, egg yolks and crème fraîche, then add this to the pan along with the basil and Parmesan. Mix in with tongs, adding a little of the cooking water, if needed, to make a creamy sauce that coats the pasta. Serve with extra Parmesan grated over the top, if you like.

Ceviche

Ingredients

500g firm white fish fillets, such as haddock, halibut or pollack, skinned and thinly sliced

juice 8 limes

(250ml/9fl oz), plus extra wedges to serve

1 red onion, sliced into rings

handful pitted green olives, finely chopped

2-3 green chillies, finely chopped

2-3 tomatoes, seeded and chopped into 2cm pieces

bunch coriander, roughly chopped

2 tbsp extra-virgin olive oil

good pinch caster sugar

tortilla chips, to serve

Method

In a large glass bowl, combine the fish, lime juice and onion. The juice should completely cover the fish; if not, add a little more. Cover with cling film and place in the fridge for 1 hr 30 mins.

Remove the fish and onion from the lime juice (discard the juice) and place in a bowl. Add the olives, chilies, tomatoes, coriander and olive oil, stir gently, then season with a good pinch of salt and sugar. This can be made a couple of hours in advance and stored in the fridge. Serve with tortilla chips to scoop up the ceviche and enjoy with a glass of cold beer.

Mushroom & thyme risotto

Ingredients

1 tbsp olive oil

350g chestnut mushrooms, sliced

100g quinoa

1l hot vegetable stock

175g risotto rice

handful of thyme leaves

handful of grated parmesan

or vegetarian alternative

50g bag rocket, to serve

Method

Heat the oil in a medium pan, sauté the mushrooms for 2-3 mins, then stir in the quinoa. Keeping the vegetable stock warm in a separate pan on a low heat, add a ladle of the stock and stir until absorbed. Stir in the rice and repeat again with the stock, until all the stock has been used up and the rice and quinoa are tender and cooked.

Stir in the thyme leaves, then divide between four plates or bowls. Serve topped with grated parmesan and rocket leaves.

Mango & passion fruit meringue roulade

Ingredients

3 large egg

175g caster sugar

1 level tsp cornflour

1 tsp malt vinegar

1 tsp vanilla extract

icing sugar, to dust

200g fat-free Greek yogurt

1 large ripe mango, peeled, stoned and diced

4 passion fruits, pulp only

icing sugar (optional) and a few physalis, to decorate

raspberry sauce, to serve (see 'Try' below)

Method

Preheat the oven to 150C/ gas 2/fan 130C. Line a 33x23cm swiss roll tin with non-stick baking parchment. Beat the egg whites with an electric whisk until frothy and doubled in bulk. Slowly whisk in the caster sugar until thick and shiny. Mix the cornflour, vinegar and vanilla extract, then whisk into the egg whites.

Spoon into the tin and level the surface carefully, so you don't push out the air. Bake for 30 minutes until the meringue surface is just firm.

Remove from the oven and cover with damp greaseproof paper for 10 minutes. Dust another sheet of greaseproof paper with icing sugar. Discard the damp paper and turn the meringue out on to the sugarcoated paper. Peel off the lining paper, then spread yogurt over the meringue and scatter with mango and passion fruit. Use the paper to roll up the roulade from one short end. Keep the join underneath. Sift a little icing sugar on top if you like, decorate with physalis and serve with raspberry sauce.

Miso brown rice & chicken salad

Ingredients

120g brown basmati rice

2 skinless chicken breasts

140g sprouting broccoli

4 spring onions, cut into diagonal slices

1 tbsp toasted sesame seeds

For the dressing

2 tsp miso paste

1 tbsp rice vinegar

1 tbsp mirin

1 tsp grated ginger

Method

Cook the rice following the pack instructions, then drain and keep warm. While it's cooking, place the chicken breasts into a pan of boiling water so they are completely covered. Boil for 1 min, then turn off the heat, place a lid on and let sit for 15 mins. When cooked through, cut into slices.

Boil the broccoli until tender. Drain, rinse under cold water and drain again.

For the dressing, mix the miso, rice vinegar, mirin and ginger together.

Divide the rice between two plates and scatter over the spring onions and sesame seeds. Place the broccoli and chicken slices on top. To finish, drizzle over the dressing.

Chicken with lemon & courgette couscous

Ingredients

200g couscous

400ml chicken stock

2 tbsp olive oil

4 courgettes, grated

2 lemons, 1 halved, 1 cut into wedges

2 boneless, skinless chicken breasts

Method

Tip the couscous into a large bowl and pour over the stock. Cover and leave for 10 mins until fluffy and all the stock has been absorbed. Heat 1 tbsp oil and fry the courgettes until softened and crisping at the edges. Tip into the couscous, then stir in with plenty of seasoning and a good squeeze of lemon juice from one of the halves.

Halve the chicken breasts horizontally and put each piece on a sheet of cling film. Cover with another sheet and beat each piece out with a rolling pin to make it thinner. Season. Heat the remaining oil in a large pan and fry the chicken for about 2 mins on each side until cooked through. Squeeze over the juice from the other lemon half and serve with the couscous and lemon wedges on the side.

Red lentil, chickpea & chilli soup

Ingredients

2 tsp cumin seeds

large pinch chilli flakes

1 tbsp olive oil

1 red onion, chopped

140g red split lentils

850ml vegetable stock or water

400g can tomatoes, whole or chopped

200g can chickpeas or ½ a can, drained and rinsed (freeze leftovers)

small bunch coriander, roughly chopped (save a few leaves, to serve)

4 tbsp 0% Greek yogurt, to serve

Method

Heat a large saucepan and dry-fry 2 tsp cumin seeds and a large pinch of chilli flakes for 1 min, or until they start to jump around the pan and release their aromas.

Add 1 tbsp olive oil and 1 chopped red onion, and cook for 5 mins.

Stir in 140g red split lentils, 850ml vegetable stock or water and a 400g can tomatoes, then bring to the boil. Simmer for 15 mins until the lentils have softened.

Whizz the soup with a stick blender or in a food processor until it is a rough purée, pour back into the pan and add a 200g can drained and rinsed chickpeas.

Heat gently, season well and stir in a small bunch of chopped coriander, reserving a few leaves to serve. Finish with 4 tbsp 0% Greek yogurt and extra coriander leaves.

Spice-rubbed chicken with pomegranate salad

Ingredients

4 skinless chicken leg joints, cut into drumsticks and thighs

2½ tsp turmeric

2½ tsp sweet paprika

½ tsp chilli flakes

2½ tsp coarsely ground black pepper

1 tbsp olive oil

3 tbsp white wine vinegar

For the salad

seeds from 1 pomegranate

3 oranges, segmented

juice ½ lime, plus extra wedges to serve

1 tbsp pomegranate molasses

small handful mint

leaves, torn

Method

Score the chicken with a sharp knife, about 2-3 cuts in each piece. Mix the spices with a little salt, the olive oil and vinegar in a small bowl. Using gloves (turmeric stains your fingers), rub this spice mixture over the chicken pieces and transfer to a roasting tin. Leave to marinate for at least 20 mins, or overnight in the fridge if you're preparing ahead.

Heat oven to 200C/180C fan/gas 6. Cover the chicken with foil and bake for 30 mins. Remove the foil and continue cooking in the oven for another 10 mins until tender. Baste with tin juices and rest for 5 mins before serving.

Meanwhile, make the salad. Mix the pomegranate seeds with the orange segments, mix the lime juice with the pomegranate molasses, then drizzle over. Scatter with torn mint leaves and serve alongside the chicken.

Spelt & wild mushroom risotto

Ingredients

200g pearled spelt

25g dried porcini mushrooms

½ tbsp olive oil

1 onion, finely diced

2 garlic cloves, finely chopped

100g chestnut button mushroom, cut into quarters

100ml white wine

1l hot vegetable stock

1 tbsp low-fat crème fraîche

bunch chives, finely chopped

handful grated pecorino or parmesan

to serve (optional)

Method

Cover the spelt with cold water and soak the dried mushrooms in 100ml boiling water in a separate bowl for 20 mins. Heat the olive oil in a large frying pan. Tip in the onion and garlic, cook for 2 mins, then add the chestnut mushrooms and cook for a further 2 mins. Drain the spelt and add along with the wine. Simmer until almost all the liquid evaporates, stirring often.

Drain the porcini mushrooms, add them to the pan and the soaking liquid to the vegetable stock. Stir in the stock 1 cup at a time and simmer, stirring often, until all liquid is absorbed and the spelt is just tender, about 20 mins in total. Stir in the crème fraîche and season with salt and pepper. Spoon onto plates and sprinkle over chives and cheese (if using).

Spicy spaghetti with garlic mushrooms

Ingredients

2 tbsp olive oil

250g pack chestnut mushroom, thickly sliced

1 garlic clove, thinly sliced

small bunch parsley, leaves only

1 celery

stick, finely chopped

1 onion, finely chopped

400g can chopped tomato

1/2 red chilli, deseeded and finely chopped, (or use drieds chilli flakes)

300g spaghetti

Method

Heat 1 tbsp oil in a pan, add the mushrooms, then fry over a high heat for 3 mins until golden and softened. Add the garlic, fry for 1 min more, then tip into a bowl with the parsley. Add the onion and celery to the pan with the rest of the oil, then fry for 5 mins until lightly coloured.

Stir in the tomatoes, chilli and a little salt, then bring to the boil. Reduce the heat and simmer, uncovered, for 10 mins until thickened. Meanwhile, boil the spaghetti, then drain. Toss with the sauce, top with the garlicky mushrooms, then serve.